89

With thanks to my loved ones,
wherever and whenever you are.

Dear Reader,

89 is best read from front to back, as you would read a novel.

89 is for Hope

Marjorie Hope Flemming
b. September 3, 1906 (Jamaica)
d. August 4, 1999 (Canada)

M. HOPE KELLY FLEMMING

NOSTALGIA

Down where Jamaica's tropic sun rides high,
Where radiant winter shines in gold and green,
In gloom of evening shadows I have seen
The tall poinsettias drip blood against the sky.
O, Canada! I love your gleaming snows,
Your wheatfields, rippling russet in the breeze, —
But how to wean a homesick heart, that knows
Where moonlight spills white magic through the trees?
Or where on long smooth beaches I may lie
On golden sands at mellow dusk, and see
The palm-trees' inky fingers etch the sky
While crimson sunsets throb across the sea.
Homage to thee, great pulsing Canada!
But, when God's vast creative work was done,
He pinned a tiny jewel to His robe —
This little island, smiling at the sun.

M. Hope Kelly Flemming.

Editorial Note: This poem was written soon after the author's marriage at which time she had to take up residence in Canada.

M. Hope Flemming 1906—1999

internationalwomensday

thebit
betweenmylegs
wheniwasborn
haseverything
andnothing
todo
withwho
iamtoday

89of89

yes

ihaveknown
enoughnos
toknow
thatno
isnever
negative

individual

wholebut
somehowhe
letsmebe

strongand
somehowhe
addstome

completeyet
somehowhe
helpsmesee

thegreaterwe

87of89

goals

excellence
livesinthe
process
theresult
holdsno
promises

tree

tree
doesnot
questionif
sheshould
be

takeroot
takespace
tremendous
tree

    85of89

homeless

he
homelessman
bagsabout
dustyclothes
shabby
nighttimetrain
lonelyplatform
brushingteeth
slowly
i
holiness
pocketreach
shinyheart
proudly
handoutstretched
billemerges
pushingforth
nobly
he
homelessman
shakeshishead
looksaway
no
i
oh

84of89

insomnia

roominmybed
armsoutstretched
alltheblankets
allthepillows
allthespace

sleepinthemiddle
noearplugs
nodreamsofchainsaws
ormotorcycles

wakenaturally
whenmybodyisready
checkmyphone
nolightdisturbs
writeinmyjournal

plantomorrow
andtomorrow
andtomorrow

but

thatlasttomorrow
youareback
soikeepspace
foryou

becausethejoysofabed
tomyself
areonlytheluxuries
oflonliness

83of89

benefitofthedoubt

you
textwhile
drivingyourcar
ridingtheescalator
walkingdownstairs
steppingoffthetrain
strollingonthesidewalk
butitispossiblethat
youarenot
entirely
evil

82of89

besties

friend
totheend
whatsup
coffeecup
cheesecake
heartbreak
havealaugh
selfiegraph
drywhitewine
genuine
wishthebest
happiness
consolethroughtears
thendisappears

forgenitallove

81of89

andrepeat

whymewhyme
ifnotyou
someoneelse
whymewhyme
ifnotyou
someoneelse
whymewhyme
ifnotyou
someoneelse
whymewhyme
ifnotyou
someoneelse
whymewhyme
ifnotyou
someoneelse

80of89

woman

shewasababy
leavingthe
womb
tookitwithher
nowher
home
iswithin

790f89

progress

somuchfusson
hypocricy
whencynicsbring
autocracy

78of89

edit

apoem
aboutlove
lovepoem
stillwriting
writingfor
thirtythree
years
cannot
quite
quite
finish

77of89

insomnia

earlymorning
aknocking
onthedoor
tomysoul

whatmessage
tonight
distanttraveler
whomakesmybody
home

whatgifts
fromimpossibleuniverses
whatwhispers
fromfingerskimmingstars

sleep
shesays
sleep

thedoor
tothebeyond
willunlock

there
wewillmeet
there
iwilltellyouall

sighence

bomb
ushard
and
whenitsdone
blast
haspushedus
awayfromthesun

orbitshift
earthtransforming

headline

warstops
globalwarming

75of89

Swept and Garnished

I deemed my bolted dwelling now secure
So lately ravaged by the storm of sin
But in the little space between the door
The winds of all the world have entered in.

Ah! While I slept, in that deep buried past,
A thousand demon-dreams possessed my brain
And day is heavy on my waking heart
For old desire is strong in me
again.

M. Hope Flemming 1906—1999

insomnia

demonspassthroughdreams
clownskartwheelcolour
facelessflashgrotesquemask
mockmyvanity
whispermyinsanity
rejectmyhumanity
nobodycares
foolishgrasping
singingwomanchild
unconditionallove
forallbutyou
stubbornoptimistgiveup
youpointlesswasteof
spaceandtime
beautywillleaveyou
sowillyourmind
loveyouwillfind
willleaveyoubehind
itsallamatteroffactandtime
wake
darknessanddemonlaughter
racingheart
tearchokedthroat
reachforlove
pillow

ascreen
myraft

dreamhardmysweet
throughthefrontlinesofmyfear
mydemonsdarenotlaugh
whenyouarenear

realistic

why
whenpeoplesay
berealistic
dotheymean
expectthe
worst

thesun
isjust
asrealas
therain

730f89

unconditional

ifyouwanttogo
iwillalways
setyoufree
because
mylove
iloveyouand
iamalso
fondof
me

72of89

stoptrying

sohard

710f89

burden

mylifeafight
insearchofspace
inbattle
withmylonging

butnow

inpeace
withinwithout
theweapons
ofbelonging

7oof89

insomnia

thosemornings
riseandshine
lookingforward
tobedtime

690f89

suffer

some
learnto
others
learnthrough

68of89

there

notquitebutgetting

670f89

unbreakable

thewristfractures
toavoid
breakingthearm
theanklefractures
toavoid
breakingtheleg
theheartfractures
toavoid
breakingthespirit

howfoolish

66of89

open

peopleliketotellme
howopentheyare
quiteopen
reallyopen
veryopen
iliketoadmire
allthespacetheyhavefound
insidetheirbox

650f89

endless

endlessemails
inmybox
whatoncesavedtime
nowparadox

640f89

endurance

awalk
atree
barkstripped
roottotip
yet
onetiredspot
holdingclinging
abranch
atwig
onesmallleaf
swinging

630f89

lifeliterally

inthetendaysi
wasawayapair
ofnestingblackbirds
builttheirnursery
onmybalcony
lifeliterally
goesonwithoutme

62of89

insideout

thenoisethechaos
mywindowblocks
protectscityears
fromprivatetalks

610f89

timemachine

chargeran
accessory

smartphone
runsontime

600f89

kthanks

heylife
itrustyou
and
iunderstand
that
nosarelessons
and
somelessons
are
harderthanothers
but
myfriendneedsayes
so
canyoureveal
the
rightyes
forher

59of89

deadofnight

blackbirds
nesting
onmyporch
nowmyjoy
nowmydelight

theproblemis
mybrainisstuckon
blackbird
singinginthe
deadofnight
blackbird
singinginthe
deadofnight
blackbird
singinginthe

iphronic

myvoicemailgreeting
says
hi
donotleaveamessage

570f89

alifeaway

thethingabout
alifeaway
is
thewishtoleave
thechoicetostay

seeing
familyeveryday
vs
seeking
spiritualdna

56of89

cupcakesnwine

because
beinganadult
mostlymeans
saying
youdid
good
toyour
owndamnedself

550f89

parenting

tinyblackbird
gainingweight
mommydaddy
workinglate
flyingsearching
dayandnightto
feedanendless
appetite

54of89

altitude

ateveryturnan
objectofbeauty
germanonhertongue
andperfectcoffee
asoulmadeoutof
curiosity
thiswomantree
becomes
thebourgeoisie

ancestorssit
atopamountainsea
theysmileandwonder
laughingsay

look
she

530f89

moment

writingpoetry
helpsme
tolive
inthe
moment
sometimes
thatmoment
istwenty
years
ago

52of89

bothsides

alittlegirl
ontheflight
askedherfather
ifshecouldgo
outside
andbounce
ontheclouds

hesaid
no
andexplained
why

she
wassad
sowas
i

        51of89

innerchild

myfavoritething
iliketosee
is
what
lightsyou
unconsciously

500f89

mindmassage

asilaystretched
onthemassagebed
atowelpillow
formyhead
mythoughtsdriftto
myfinalhour
mydyingbreath
myfuneralbower

whenwillitbe
myfinalword
whenwill
myfinalbreathbeheard
myfinalkiss
myfinaltouch
my

perhaps
ithink
ondeath
toomuch

49of89

emptynest

silently
nofuss
nomess
theblackbirds
haveleftthenest
onmybalcony

nowiwatch
thecitybirds
moreclosely
searchingfor
mylittlefamily
hoping
secretly
thatthey
recogniseme

480f89

squirrel

whensomeone
tellsmetheir
spiritanimal
isa
catdoglionwolf
orbutterfly
iwondersadly
whatorwho
killedtheir
imagination

470f89

cheapass

sometimes
isitincafes
writingpoetry
lookingatmyphone
occasionally
checkingthedoor
expectantly
sighingheavily
pretendingtobe
stoodup
then
leavingsuddenly
soidonothavetobuy
athreeeuro
cupof
coffee

message

sometimes
shewhispers
sometimes
shescreams
that
all
is
exactly
asitseems

450f89

soulmate

withyou
my
soulhas
finallylost
itsvirginity

440f89

freewill

somucheffort
makingdecisions
onlytolearn
therewas
never
any
choice

430f89

lifereflecting

sidewalks
bloomingwith
cigarettebutts
as
dandelions
ingreenfields
before

420f89

colourtime

if
numbers
onaclock
tellme
only
thatimustnow
speedup
slowdown
orstop

iwonder
whywecannot
measuretime
in
colour

410f89

relativity

poor
unconscious
humanity
saidthe
tree

400f89

adultslide

fridaynightslikethis
goodwine
ontheside
freedaynightsofbliss
dinnertalk
satisfied
cleverconversation
noneedto
gooutside

hey

doesanyoneremember
theelectric
slide

390f89

palette

neitherpainter
norpainting
she
wasthe
palette

38of89

lightyears

themoment
youget
her
sheis
alreadygone

   37of89

lostroot

tree
wearyandworn
onhisknees
lipstoearth
whispered

root
youmust
letgo
again

36of89

thanks

thesky
isnotbothered
ifyoucomplain
so
putonahat
andthank
therain

35of89

infearitance

oneday
uponwaking
insomniasdaughter
knew
herfears
werenot
hers
butfromwhat
hadbeentaughther

34of89

lifesoup

asprinkle
ofsorrow
addsflavour
complexity

forsurely
somesadness
ispartof
therecipe

      330f89

seadreams

starssnuggle
eyesblinking
beneath
blanketwaves
frigatebirdsdoze
headsheavy
between
cushionclouds
thesunyawns
teethbrushed
withpalmtrees

    32of89

eurydisea

whilethey
madeloveonshorelines
andmadelifeinrivers
whilethey
whisperedsecretsinlakes
andgrewoldinoceans

thefallenwind
watched
lonelywithgrief
ragingwithjealousy
he
begged
clawedandpulled
thecoy
sea

butshe

withherheart
inpeaceandpieces
wouldalwaysreturn
totheland
fromabove
indrenchingrain
andtorrentsoflove

31of89

mydemon 1of5

therehadbeen
nosurprisevisits
forawhile
so
lastnight
ichangedthegame
and
went
heartinhand
tosee

mydemon

close
ifoundhim
inhisdarkness
therealone
alonesitting
headbowed
inhishome
tuckedbehind
myright
ear

30of89

mydemon 2of5

istartledhim
inhisdarkness
helookedatme
facetwisted
nolaughter
only
shrinking
silence

eyeslocked
ispoke
howareyou
youarehow
hemocked
voice
alashingwhip
then
silence

29of89

mydemon 3of5

heartinhand
armoutstretched
isaid
ibroughtyouthis
thisyoubroughti
hemocked
voice
ofbrokenglass

myheart
hetook
withoutalook
and
likeasnake
ate
gulp
silence

28of89

mydemon 4of5

myheart
nowpumped
inthestomach
ofmydemon

more
hefinallywhispered
voice
ofshreddedsouls
eyesblack
hookedhands
pressed
toabellyneverfull
more

no
isaid
voicebreaking
thatisallihave
haveiallisthat
hemocked

silence

27of89

mydemon 5of5

asiturnedtoleave
more
mydemon
blackeyesnowbegging
more
hookedhandsgrasping
more
withavoice
ofahundreddaysofhunger
ofathousandnightsoflonliness
ofamillionyearsoftears
ofaneternityoffear
more

no
isaid
voicefirm
myheartisallihave
myheartisenough
icannotfeedyou
anymore

silence

epilogue

lastnight
mydemon
reappeared
blackeyes
swirlingbloodred
hookedhands
dragginglongveins
belly
stretchedpregnantfull
silencebroken
bythebeating
ofmyeverexpanding
heart

mymouthopened
toscreamlaughsing
when
hecrawledin
pastlipstongueteeth
downmythroat
deepintomychest
where
hefinallycurledup
torest

25of89

hummingbird

hummingbird
hummingbird
sizeofmythumb
bornasajewel
achildofthesun
yoursipofnectar
ismysipofrum
soundtrackisbusy
backbeatahum
nightserenade
sweetsteelpanstrum
youvisitflowers
likeivisitcoun
triesontheplanet
toearnmyincome
hummingbird
hummingbird
sizeofmythumb
alwaysreturn
wherewefamilyfrom

24of89

mybike

ilovemybike
icallitmyhorse
heasksneitherstable
norwishfordivorce

230f89

stillfighting

atseventeen
mygrandfatherfought
tohelpsetpeople
free
onehundredyearslater
mygrandfathersthoughts
arestillalive
inme

22of89

begendings

youneverknowifthis
willbeyour
finalkiss
so
liveyour
lifereversed
makeeachkissyourfirst

210f89

ubu

themoreilove
thelessicare
themoreilove

200f89

flight

iswear
theladynexttome
justsneezed
adozentimes

shedidnot
coverupherface
justlet
theliquidsfly

theonlything
tocomeofit
besidesthe
sprayandslime

isthatihadmy
journalclose
(heldupagainst
theflyinggross)
towrite
thislittlerhyme

19of89

flightpitch

ithoughtthelady
nexttome
wantedtobe
myfriend
afterachat
shetoldmethat

shesoldsupplements
bestbrandinthecountry
verygoodfordryskin
orwomensissues
wouldiliketotry
afreesample
perhapssomething
formymother
hereismy
brochure

theend

easttowest

fromseatseventeen
iseethedutchshore
theklmlogo
onthewingbythedoor
theskyaskyblue
thecloudscloudywhite
thesuspendedsunset
thedawdlingnight

17of89

goalsetting

ifyoufeelguilt
ortroubledby
constant
procrastination
perhapsstopping
tosmellthatrose
wasthetrue
destination

16of89

family

ifyoucometovisit
andmyhouse
isamess
itmeans
youarefamily
notjustaguest

15of89

prepitaph

letitbesaid
thatshe
huggedwithherheart
rememberedyourstories
spokeonlytruth

letitbesaid
shewas
kindredwithtrees
worshippedthesun
butadoredthemoon

letitbesaid
thatalthough
shewassolitary
shewantedyourcompany
andbakedcookiesastherapy

letitbesaid
thatshe
sangfromhersoul
soughttoconnect
butbelievedinlettinggo

letitbesaid
beforeherdaysaredone
thatshe
carriedlifelightly
fearednothingandnoone
andwasloved

thirteen

atthirteen
mybones
suddenly
grewfaster
andthough
ididnot
break
asingleone
something
insidemysoul
receiveda
fracture
andallatonce
ifeltiwas
alone

tofillthecrack
music
becamethe
plaster

13of89

familiar

sosimilar
toyoubigbrother
thatwhenipause
iknowyourthoughts
andwhenilook
youaremyother
evenfivethousand
milesaway

oppositepaths
oneartonescience
sosometimes
conversationsfraught
yetstillilove
acrossthesilence
youandicups
fromthesameclay

12of89

inspiralation

sometimes
thepoem
doesnotcome
andsoisit
andstare

mymind
ablank
mypen
undone
wordstangledinmyhair

11of89

calligraphy

agiantpencil
inyourhand
leadpressingpaper
untilitrips
atroopoflines
drawninthesand
beachlitteredwith
thebrokentips
apenabrush
refineyourskill
acursiveloop
nowrowonrow
tomarktheboundary
ofgoodwill
andlearntheart
ofsaying
no

10of89

resolution

aroundthesun
anotheryear
resolvetorun
isinsincere

90f89

full

sistermoon
flush
withlove
showsherfull
facetotheworld
radiantsunravished
inafterglow
andagain
again
earth
turns
away

again

energy

atthesweet
ageofseven
icouldnot
sitdown
jump
fromthesofa
run
roundandround
annoy
mypoorfamily
upset
myfriends

ihope
imthesame
atseventyten

7of89

littlemiss

ialwaysthought
thaticouldnot
miss
thatwhich
ididneverknow

nowisuspect
imincorrect
i
havenotlost
butcantletgo

6of89

To My Pen

Why have you so forsaken me, my friend,
Now when the day declines, and the dank earth
Offers cold welcome--when the power to bend
Words to my meaning pleads anew for birth?
Is there, in the vague welter of my mind,
No special joy, no grief encapsulate,
No pleasing, noble thinking I may find,
And, by your aid, render articulate?

Yet, should you join me, in my brain would surge
Venom and rage and shock, engulfed in tears;
And from its withered uterus emerge
Only the frustrate wisdom of the years.
Lie still, remote, my friend, for this is best;
Let it remain unsired, unexpressed.

M. Hope Flemming 1906—1999

oya

she
comesatnight
orwith
earlymorning
rain
hervoiceis
lowyet
shescreams
atwindow
pane

she
tearstheocean
ripstheland
agoddess
wild
deranged

hernameis
oya
she
unleashedby
climate
change

player

hesaidhewasaplayer
withatwinkleinhiseye
itwinkledbackandaskedhim
ifheeverwonderedwhy
hesaidbecauseitseasy
hesaidbecausehecan
hesaidbecauseheshorny
hesaidcuzhesaman
hesaiditgavehimsomething
funtodowhileatthegym
hesaidbecausetheladies
well
theydidthesametohim
hesaidbecausehisgirlfriend
hadtornhisheartintwo
hesaidbecausetoloveagain
wasdifficulttodo
hesaidbecausehelikesit
becausehelikesthechase
andthenhesaid
sotellme
wannacomebackto
myplace

4of89

insomnia

sleepescapesme
slippingthroughmyeyelids
divingfrommylashes
bouncingoffmycheeks
lookingfor
thecat

3of89

DARK

Camilla sees
A shaft of moonlight linger
Among the shadows in her narrow room;
Then, slow-departing, like a beckoning finger,
Leave only gloom.

Camilla hears
A train approach the hollow,
And its long siren pierce the wall of night.
Speed-polished wheels no yearning foot can follow
Impel its flight.

Camilla knows
Her eyes must ~~xixx~~ hold from weeping,
Though leaden hours weigh down upon her heart.
Waiting the sombre dawn she lies unsleeping;
Alone, apart...

M. Hope Flemming 1906—1999

motherland

runninghands
overshells
collectedclinking
solidsmooth
fromalltheshores
oceans
rivers
seas
thaticall
home

motherofpearl
oncecradled
softbodied
souls
nowshines
amongstthe
multitude
amemory

iam
still
iam
here

ideabeyond

ibegin
whereiend
chartingapath
setathousandyears
beforethoughtwasan
idea
wherewe
loversoftrees
craftersoffire
artistsonlyoflife
sangwithnodesire
beyond
asoftbed
afullbelly
astarfilledsky
yetbusywithboxes
stuckinscreens
miredinpride
idrift
dreamingofwarmroots
embracedbylove
endingwhere
ibegin

1of89

motivation

I am a woman of many lands and cultures: Trinidad & Tobago, Canada, England and The Netherlands. I have seen a lot and come to understand a lot about life, love, culture, identity, and humanity. I have written poetry my whole life and had wanted to write a series of poems for a long time, but I couldn't quite decide on the form or theme. Then, I turned 40 in the same year that Trump was elected President of the United States, and my poetry became at once a life-affirming shout and a political protest.

I first aimed to write 1000 poems. Then 100. Then 50. Seems I almost gave up before I even began. Then I recalled 89 Shepherd Rd; the street I grew up on in Halifax, Nova Scotia, Canada. Yes. 89. More romantic than 50 or 100. Personal. Achievable. It tripped easily off the tongue. So, 89 it was.

(un)planned

On International Women's Day,
8 March, 2017, I began writing 89.
This date was purely coincidental
yet completely predestined as, I
believe, are all auspicious events
in life. I completed 89 nearly
one year later on Valentine's
Day, 14 February, 2018. Another
predestined coincidence.

I wrote 89 starting from the
top and worked my way down
to number 1. I thought having
a countdown would help me to
complete the task. This mental trick
worked and I love the fact that I
can knowingly outwit myself.

muse

89 follows my life in one year: starting in The Netherlands and following my travels throughout Europe, Jamaica, Trinidad, Canada, and back to The Netherlands. 89 was inspired by my roots which run deep and wide. I learned while writing 89 that my deceased grandmother (Marjorie) Hope Flemming had also been a published poet. She was a Jamaican who also found herself in the "foreign" land of Canada. Through 89 I discovered that I had inherited my grandmother's themes, and, I believe, her memories and voice. Four of her works are included as images in 89.

89 started as fragments of previously written poems but quickly developed into a reflection on real-time events. It can look like a book of haiku but the poems are a mix of styles influenced by Rumi, Hafiz, Shakespeare, Cummings, and van den Koppel. However, like haiku, 89 became a meditative practice.

form

89 is best read from front to back as you would read a novel. The poems were originally written to be posted on Instagram so they had to be short in order to fit the screen. I write in a style I call #hashtype. I like how hashtags, like mini poems, make you stop for a moment to try to decode them. That is how I hope the reader experiences 89. Each #hashtype poem is at first only a shape, then a jumble of letters, then words, then sentences, then finally meaning, which, once perceived, allows you to then withdraw to see again the shape.

If you take your time, you can dive in again and look for single-word lines within the poem where you will often find the tiny essence of meaning. Just so, 89 touches on the many layers and aspects of my own identity and experience without any one claiming dominance.

copyright © 2018 by Nicole Jordan
copyright © 1906—1999 unpublished
poems by Hope Flemming
all rights reserved

second edition 2019
first edition 2018

design concept
Nicole Jordan

graphic care
NM studio

ISBN: 978-1-9992951-0-3

www.nicolejordan.info

www.ingramcontent.com/pod-product-compliance
Lightning Source LLC
Chambersburg PA
CBHW060404080526
44583CB00012B/468